Side Hustle to Main Hustle

Side Hustle to Main Hustle

TURNING PASSION INTO
PROFIT

B. Vincent

QuillQuest Publishers

Contents

1

Chapter 1: Introduction

Characterizing Second job and Fundamental Hustle

In our cutting edge universe of different vocation ways and pioneering adventures, it's fundamental to comprehend the nuanced contrasts between a part time job and a principal hustle. A second job addresses those purposeful ventures, innovative undertakings, or pay creating exercises sought after close by an essential kind of revenue or occupation. These undertakings frequently come from individual interests, leisure activities, or abilities that people are energetic about investigating further.

On the other hand, a principal hustle epitomizes the essential kind of revenue or vocation center that regularly requests most of one's significant investment. It might include conventional work, maintaining a business, or whatever other movement that fills in as the essential monetary spine of a singular's life.

The differentiation between these two hustles lies in their transient portion as well as in their motivation and importance inside the more extensive setting of individual and expert satisfaction. While the principal hustle gives solidness and monetary security, the part time job offers an innovative outlet, a method for self-articulation, and a road for seeking after interests past the bounds of conventional business.

Understanding the elements of part time jobs and principal hustles is crucial as we leave on the excursion of transforming enthusiasm into benefit. It makes way for investigating how these double pursuits can orchestrate, supplement, and ultimately unite to shape a satisfying and prosperous profession direction. Thus, we should dig further into the universe of side gigs, fundamental hustles, and the groundbreaking force of adjusting energy to benefit.

Significance of Transforming Energy into Benefit

In our current reality where the customary vocation direction is going through fast change, there's a developing acknowledgment of the significance of adjusting one's enthusiasm to their method for work. Transforming energy into benefit isn't just an in vogue idea; it's a basic change by they way we see work, satisfaction, and achievement.

At the point when we take part in exercises that resound with our interests, we tap into a wellspring of inspiration, imagination, and satisfaction. Energy implants our work with energy and excitement, moving us to beat obstructions and endure despite difficulties. It changes everyday errands into valuable open doors for development and development, encouraging a feeling of direction that rises above money related gain.

Additionally, seeking after our interests can prompt more noteworthy degrees of fulfillment and satisfaction in our lives. By diverting our energies into exercises that we really appreciate and see as significant, we develop a feeling of satisfaction that stretches out past monetary prizes. We get fulfillment from the actual excursion, savoring the most common way of picking up, developing, and making esteem in arrangement with our most profound interests and values.

Be that as it may, maybe in particular, transforming energy into benefit holds the possibility to open new roads of chance and success. In reality as we know it where imagination, advancement, and specialty aptitude are progressively esteemed, adapting our interests opens ways to different revenue sources, pioneering adventures, and capricious profession ways. It permits us to cut out specialties for ourselves in serious business sectors, separate our contributions, and make esteem that resounds with our interest group.

Fundamentally, the excursion from enthusiasm to benefit isn't just about monetary profit; about creating a day to day existence mirrors our genuine selves, satisfies our most profound yearnings, and leaves an enduring effect on the world. It's tied in with embracing the extraordinary force of enthusiasm and saddling it to make a vocation that is both worthwhile and profoundly significant. Thus, as we leave on this excursion together, let us notice the call to transform our interests into our most noteworthy resources and fashion a way to success powered by reason and enthusiasm.

Outline of the Excursion from Second job to Fundamental Hustle

Leaving on the excursion from second job to fundamental hustle is likened to heading out on a journey of self-disclosure, business venture, and self-awareness. It's an excursion set apart by exciting bends in the road, wins and hardships, as we explore the waters of chance, vulnerability, and desire.

At its center, this excursion is tied in with changing a meaningful venture or beneficial revenue stream into a flourishing, economical endeavor that shapes the foundation of our expert character and monetary prosperity. It's tied in with taking the seeds of imagination, resourcefulness, and enthusiasm established in our part time jobs and supporting them into prospering organizations that exemplify our vision, values, and desires.

The excursion unfurls in unmistakable stages, each described by its own difficulties, achievements, and open doors for development. It starts with the commencement of a part time job — a flash of motivation, a thought ready to be understood, an energy ready to be released. We dunk our toes into the waters of business venture, testing the practicality of our thoughts, refining our contributions, and gathering speed as we draw in our most memorable clients and clients.

As our side gig gets forward movement and energy, we wind up at an intersection — a vital snapshot of choice and opportunity. We should choose whether to keep stepping the natural waters of parttime business venture or to outline a course towards full-time quest for our enthusiasm. This change from part time job to fundamental hustle addresses an act of pure trust — a striking statement of obligation to our fantasies, our vision, and our true capacity for progress.

However, the excursion doesn't end there. With the change to full-opportunity business venture comes another arrangement of difficulties and obligations. We should explore the intricacies of scaling our business, dealing with our assets, and adjusting to the requests of a dynamic and cutthroat commercial center. We should develop flexibility, versatility, and a development outlook as we experience misfortunes, impediments, and unexpected difficulties en route.

At last, the excursion from part time job to fundamental hustle is a demonstration of the force of energy, persistence, and reason. It's an excursion of self-revelation and discipline, of innovativeness and development, of hazard and prize. Furthermore, as we leave on this excursion together, let us embrace the potential open doors it presents, gain from its difficulties, and commend the triumphs — both of all shapes and sizes — that look for us on the way to transforming energy into benefit.

Laying out Objectives and Assumptions for the Book

As we leave on this extraordinary excursion from side gig to fundamental hustle, it's fundamental to lay out clear objectives and assumptions for what lies ahead. This book fills in as a directing light — a guide for exploring the difficulties, quickly jumping all over the chances, and opening the maximum capacity of our pioneering tries.

Most importantly, we want to outfit you with the information, devices, and systems you really want to transform your energy into benefit. Whether you're a sprouting business person with a side gig in its outset or an accomplished entrepreneur hoping to take your dare to a higher level, this book is intended to give useful bits of knowledge, significant counsel, and demonstrated methods for progress.

Our point is to demystify the most common way of incorporating an effective side gig and progressing it into an undeniable principal hustle. We'll dig into key points, for example, distinguishing your enthusiasm, arranging your business, constructing your image, overseeing funds, scaling your activity, and conquering difficulties en route. Through true models, contextual analyses, and master bits of knowledge, we'll enlighten the way ahead and engage you to explore the intricacies of business with certainty and clearness.

Yet, past simple functional direction, we want to rouse and enable you to seek after your fantasies with mental fortitude, conviction, and unflinching assurance. We accept that every one of us has the possibility to make an existence of direction, satisfaction, and flourishing by adjusting our interests to our expert interests. What's more, through the pages of this book, we desire to light the flash of plausibility inside you — to encourage you to think beyond practical boundaries, make an intense move, and graph a course towards a future characterized by energy, reason, and benefit.

Thus, as you submerge yourself in the pages that follow, we urge you to move toward this excursion with a receptive outlook, a willing heart, and a feeling of experience. Put forth clear objectives for what you desire to accomplish, and cling tightly to the assumption that with devotion, persistence, and a faith in yourself, the sky is the limit. Together, let us set out on this uncommon excursion of change and revelation, as we transform our interests into our most noteworthy resources and manufacture a way to progress in our own particular manner.

2

Chapter 2: Discovering Your Passion

Recognizing Your Inclinations and Abilities

In the mission to transform your energy into benefit, the initial step is to set out on an excursion of self-revelation — to investigate the immense scene of your inclinations, leisure activities, and abilities looking for that slippery flash that lights your spirit. This cycle isn't only about recognizing what you appreciate or what you're great at; about uncovering the interests resound profoundly inside you — the pursuits that fill you with a feeling of direction, satisfaction, and happiness.

To start this investigation, we'll set out on a progression of activities and reflection prompts intended to strip back the layers of your character and uncover the center interests that lie underneath. We'll dive into your inclinations, side interests, and hobbies, examining underneath the surface to reveal the exercises that present to you the best fulfillment and satisfaction. We'll investigate your abilities and gifts, focusing on the areas where you succeed and the qualities that put you aside.

As you participate in these activities, permit yourself to dream without impediments — to imagine a future where your interests are side interests or hobbies as well as the main impetus behind your job.

Consider the exercises that empower you, the difficulties that move you, and the minutes when time appears to stop as you drench yourself in your picked interest. These are the pieces of information — the bread-crumbs that will lead you nearer to the core of your enthusiasm and the way to transforming it into benefit.

However, recollect, self-revelation isn't an objective; it's an excursion — a persistent course of investigation, development, and advancement. As you uncover new interests, foster new abilities, and experience new open doors, permit yourself to embrace the consistently changing scene of your interests and yearnings. Remain inquisitive, remain receptive, or more all, remain consistent with yourself as you explore the invigorating territory of finding your energy and manufacturing a way to thriving.

Understanding the Market Interest for Your Energy

While distinguishing your interests is an essential initial step, the excursion from enthusiasm to benefit requires a more profound comprehension of the commercial center wherein you plan to work. In this section, we'll set out on an excursion of market investigation — a mission to uncover the interest for your energy and survey its likely practicality as a type of revenue.

To start, we'll dive into research techniques pointed toward assessing market interest inside your picked specialty. We'll investigate procedures for social event information, dissecting patterns, and evaluating customer conduct to acquire bits of knowledge into the necessities, wants, and inclinations of your ideal interest group. By understanding the market scene, you'll be better prepared to distinguish open doors for advancement, separation, and worth creation inside your specialty.

As we explore the complexities of market investigation, we'll likewise focus on the opposition — inspecting the methodologies, contributions, and situating of existing players inside your specialty. By concentrating on the cutthroat scene, you'll acquire significant bits of knowledge into industry standards, client assumptions, and possible holes or amazing open doors that might exist inside the market.

Yet, statistical surveying isn't just about information and investigation; it's likewise about instinct and sympathy — about grasping the human component that underlies purchaser conduct. All through this section, we'll urge you to place yourself in the shoes of your interest group — to identify with their requirements, wants, and trouble spots — and to imagine how your enthusiasm can act as an answer or wellspring of significant worth in their lives.

Eventually, the objective of understanding business sector request is to illuminate and direct your decision-production as you leave on the excursion of adapting your energy. Furnished with experiences into the necessities and inclinations of your interest group, you'll be better prepared to tailor your contributions, refine your advertising procedures, and position your image for progress in the commercial center. Thus, as we dig into the complexities of market investigation, let us approach this section with interest, receptiveness, and a readiness to uncover the secret open doors that exist in the domain of our interests.

Investigating Various Roads for Adapting Your Energy

With an unmistakable comprehension of your inclinations and the market interest for your enthusiasm, now is the ideal time to investigate the different roads through which you can change your energy into benefit. In this part, we'll set out on an excursion of pioneering investigation, revealing the heap manners by which you can adapt your gifts, abilities, and skill.

We'll start by acquainting you with different adaptation methodologies, going from conventional item deals to present day computerized adventures. Whether you're making carefully assembled merchandise, offering specific administrations, or making computerized items, there are endless ways of producing pay from your enthusiasm. Through true models and contextual analyses, we'll enlighten the potential outcomes and motivate you to ponder how you can use your enthusiasm to make esteem in the commercial center.

As we investigate these various roads for adaptation, we'll likewise dig into the functional contemplations engaged with building a productive business around your energy. From estimating methodologies and income models to dissemination channels and deals strategies, we'll furnish you with the information and instruments you want to explore the intricacies of business and expand your procuring potential.

In any case, adapting your enthusiasm isn't just about bringing in cash — it's tied in with making significant associations with your crowd and having a constructive outcome in their lives. All through this part, we'll accentuate the significance of adjusting your adaptation methodology to your qualities, objectives, and yearnings. By remaining consistent with yourself and your vision, you'll construct a productive business as well as develop a reliable local area of clients who share your enthusiasm and value the worth you give.

Along these lines, as we set out on this excursion of pioneering disclosure, let us approach every road for adapting our enthusiasm with interest, inventiveness, and a receptive outlook. Whether you decide to sell items, offer administrations, or make computerized content, recollect that the conceivable outcomes are inestimable — and that with devotion, assurance, and a promise to greatness, you can transform your enthusiasm into a flourishing business that gives pleasure, satisfaction, and thriving to both yourself and your clients.

Activities and Exercises to Pinpoint Your Enthusiasm

Chasing transforming your energy into benefit, it's fundamental to take part in organized activities and exercises that work with the disclosure and refinement of your center advantages. This part will direct you through a progression of reasonable activities intended to pinpoint your enthusiasm, explain your objectives, and adjust your goals to substantial business thoughts.

We'll begin by empowering you to ponder your previous encounters, leisure activities, and interests, testing underneath the surface to uncover the exercises that light your excitement and fuel your inventiveness. Through directed prompts and thoughtful activities, you'll acquire further experiences into the interests that resound most emphatically with you and the expected roads for transforming them into beneficial endeavors.

Then, we'll investigate methods for setting explicit, quantifiable, reachable, significant, and time-bound (Savvy) objectives for your enterprising excursion. By articulating clear targets and achievements, you'll make a guide for progress and graph a course toward understanding your vision of transforming energy into benefit.

All through this part, you'll likewise have the chance to conceptualize and create business thoughts that influence your interests and line up with market interest. Whether you're keen on beginning an item based business, offering specific administrations, or making computerized content, we'll give direction and backing to assist you with recognizing promising open doors and evaluate their plausibility.

At long last, we'll offer viable ways to remain persuaded and zeroed in as you set out on the excursion of business. From developing a development outlook to embracing disappointment as a learning a valuable open door, we'll outfit you with the mentality and instruments you want to explore the unavoidable difficulties and misfortunes that go with the quest for your energy.

By participating in these activities and exercises, you'll explain your energy and business objectives as well as gain the certainty and lucidity to make an unequivocal move toward transforming your fantasies into the real world. Thus, as you drench yourself during the time spent pinpointing your enthusiasm, make sure to move toward each activity with a receptive outlook, a feeling of interest, and an eagerness to embrace the groundbreaking force of business venture.

3

∾

Chapter 3: Planning Your Side Hustle

Laying out Shrewd Objectives for Your Second job

In the thrilling excursion of sending off a side gig, laying out clear and key objectives is much the same as plotting a seminar on a navigational guide — it gives guidance, center, and a feeling of direction. In this part, we'll plunge profound into the workmanship and study of objective setting, acquainting you with the Savvy system — an incredible asset for making objectives that are Explicit, Quantifiable, Feasible, Pertinent, and Time-bound.

Explicitness is the foundation of viable objective setting. By articulating definitively what you intend to accomplish with your part time job, you make a guide for progress that rules out vagueness or vulnerability. Whether it's rising income, extending your client base, or sending off another product offering, characterizing explicit objectives empowers you to channel your endeavors and assets toward significant results.

Quantifiability is fundamental for following advancement and assessing achievement. By laying out clear measurements and achievements to check your presentation, you gain important experiences into the adequacy of your systems and the regions where improvement is required.

Whether it's deals targets, site traffic, or client commitment measurements, quantifiable objectives give unmistakable benchmarks to progress.

Attainability guarantees that your objectives are reachable and lined up with your assets, capacities, and limitations. While it's crucial for reach skyward and think beyond practical boundaries, defining objectives that are reasonably feasible cultivates a feeling of certainty and inspiration, enabling you to make an unequivocal move and gain consistent headway toward your goals.

Pertinence is tied in with guaranteeing that your objectives line up with your more extensive vision, values, and desires. By interfacing your second job objectives to your own and proficient goals, you make a feeling of arrangement and reason that powers your energy and responsibility. Whether it's propelling your profession, chasing after your enthusiasm, or accomplishing monetary autonomy, applicable objectives resound profoundly with your guiding principle and inspirations.

Time-bound objectives make a need to keep moving and responsibility, driving you to make a steady move and gain significant headway toward your targets. By laying out clear cutoff times and timetables for accomplishing your objectives, you make a feeling of energy and center that drives you forward, even notwithstanding hindrances and difficulties.

All through this section, we'll give useful direction, models, and formats to assist you with creating Brilliant objectives that drive your second job forward and change your desires into substantial results. Thus, as you set out on this excursion of objective setting, make sure to move toward each step with deliberateness, clearness, and a pledge to greatness. By defining Shrewd objectives for your part time job, you'll make ready for progress and open the maximum capacity of your pioneering tries.

Making a Marketable strategy and Spending plan

In the domain of business venture, a very much created field-tested strategy and spending plan act as the bedrock whereupon fruitful endeavors are fabricated. In this section, we dig into the fundamental parts of making a complete strategy and financial plan for your second job, giving you the devices, bits of knowledge, and systems to explore the intricacies of pioneering arranging with certainty and clearness.

We'll start by investigating the life structures of a marketable strategy — a vital guide that frames your objectives, target market, items or administrations, showcasing methodology, and monetary projections. By carefully itemizing every part of your side gig, you'll acquire a more profound comprehension of your business' main goal, vision, and incentive, making way for informed direction and vital execution.

Then, we'll direct you through the most common way of leading statistical surveying and examination to distinguish your main interest group, evaluate contender contributions, and reveal open doors for separation and worth creation. Furnished with bits of knowledge into market elements and customer inclinations, you'll be better prepared to situate your side gig for progress and gain by arising patterns and potential open doors inside your specialty.

As we investigate the complexities of business arranging, we'll likewise focus on the significance of monetary administration and planning. By making a point by point spending plan that records for costs, income projections, and income the board, you'll establish the groundwork for monetary maintainability and versatility, moderating dangers and vulnerabilities that might emerge along the innovative excursion.

All through this section, we'll give reasonable tips, layouts, and guides to assist you with drafting a marketable strategy and spending plan that lines up with your objectives, desires, and assets. Whether you're looking for subsidizing, drawing in financial backers, or basically graphing a course for your pioneering tries, a very much created strategy and spending plan will act as priceless devices for directing your navigation and driving your second job toward progress.

Thus, as you set out on the excursion of making a strategy and spending plan for your part time job, make sure to move toward each step with steadiness, inventiveness, and a pledge to greatness. By establishing serious areas of strength for a point for your endeavor, you'll get yourself positioned for long haul achievement and open the maximum capacity of your enterprising goals.

Overseeing Time Actually to Adjust Your Fundamental Hustle and Side gig

As you explore the unique scene of business, excelling at using time productively is fundamental to keeping up with equilibrium and congruity between your principal hustle, second job, and individual life. In this part, we'll investigate systems and methods for streamlining your time, augmenting efficiency, and shuffling different obligations with effortlessness and effectiveness.

We'll start by accentuating the significance of prioritization — distinguishing the undertakings and exercises that are generally crucial for the outcome of your side gig and assigning your significant investment likewise. By zeroing in on high-influence exercises and limiting interruptions, you'll guarantee that you take advantage of your restricted time and accomplish significant advancement toward your objectives.

Then, we'll dive into the idea of defining limits — a basic yet frequently neglected part of compelling using time effectively. Whether it's laying out devoted work hours, assigning explicit days for side gig exercises, or cutting out time for taking care of oneself and unwinding, defining limits permits you to safeguard your time, energy, and prosperity, guaranteeing that you keep a good overall arrangement between your expert and individual responsibilities.

As we investigate the complexities of using time productively, we'll likewise acquaint you with procedures for boosting efficiency and conquering normal deterrents like dawdling, overpower, and burnout. From time-hindering and bunch handling to executing efficiency apparatuses and methods, you'll figure out how to smooth out your work process, limit interruptions, and achieve more quicker than expected.

In any case, successful time usage isn't just about efficiency — it's additionally about saving your psychological and profound prosperity as you explore the requests of business venture. All through this part, we'll underline the significance of taking care of oneself, stress the executives, and keeping a solid balance between fun and serious activities. By focusing on rest, unwinding, and amusement, you'll re-energize your batteries, recharge your imagination, and support the energy and excitement expected to flourish in the quick moving universe of business.

In this way, as you leave on the excursion of dealing with your time successfully to adjust your primary hustle and side gig, make sure to move toward every day with purposefulness, discipline, and a pledge to taking care of oneself. By excelling at using time productively, you'll not just make more prominent efficiency and progress in your enterprising undertakings yet additionally develop a day to day existence that is rich, satisfying, and adjusted in each perspective.

Methodologies for Defeating Normal Difficulties and Misfortunes

In the erratic landscape of business venture, difficulties and misfortunes are unavoidable buddies on the excursion toward progress. In this section, we'll investigate commonsense procedures and attitude movements to assist you with exploring the deterrents and afflictions that might emerge as you seek after your side gig desires.

We'll start by distinguishing normal difficulties looked by side hawkers, like time imperatives, monetary restrictions, and self-question. By recognizing these obstructions forthright, you'll be more ready to expect and address them proactively, limiting their effect on your advancement and resolve.

Then, we'll dig into down to earth methodologies for conquering these difficulties and mishaps. From utilizing your assets and assets to looking for help from coaches, peers, and online networks, you'll find an abundance of devices and methods for versatility and transformation even with misfortune.

All through this section, we'll likewise stress the significance of developing a development mentality — a confidence in your capacity to learn, develop, and defeat impediments through steadiness and exertion. By reexamining misfortunes as any open doors for learning and development, you'll change difficulty into a springboard for individual and expert turn of events, impelling you nearer to your objectives and desires.

As we investigate these methodologies for defeating difficulties, we'll draw motivation from genuine models and examples of overcoming adversity of people who have explored obstructions to fabricate flourishing part time jobs. By gaining from their encounters and experiences, you'll acquire important insight and viewpoint to apply to your own enterprising excursion.

In this way, as you experience difficulties and mishaps on the way to transforming your energy into benefit, recall that flexibility, determination, and a positive mentality are your most prominent resources. By embracing the inescapable high points and low points of business with boldness and assurance, you'll arise more grounded, savvier, and stronger than at any other time. Also, with every deterrent you survive, you'll inch nearer to understanding your fantasies and making the progress you merit.

4

Chapter 4: Building Your Brand

Characterizing Your Own Image and One of a kind Selling Suggestion

In the clamoring commercial center of business, where rivalry is savage and capacities to focus are brief, the idea of individual marking arises as a reference point of differentiation — a method for cutting out a remarkable character and standing apart in the midst of the commotion. In this part, we set out on an excursion of self-disclosure and separation, investigating the subtleties of individual marking and the crucial job it plays in the progress of your side gig.

At its quintessence, individual marking is tied in with articulating what your identity is, a big motivator for you, and why you matter — a true articulation of your qualities, interests, and skill that reverberates with your interest group. By characterizing your own image, you make a strong story that separates you from contenders, lays out believability and trust, and develops a devoted following of clients and allies.

Be that as it may, individual marking goes past simple self-advancement or advertising — it's tied in with revealing the substance of what makes you exceptional and utilizing it to make an incentive for other people. To start this excursion of self-disclosure, we'll direct you through a course of contemplation and reflection, empowering you to investigate your center assets, values, and character qualities that separate you from others in your field.

Then, we'll dig into the idea of the interesting selling recommendation (USP) — an unmistakable incentive that typifies what separates your side gig and why clients ought to pick you over contenders. By recognizing your USP, you'll take shape your offer and lucid it in a manner that reverberates with your ideal interest group, convincing them to draw in with your image and backing your business.

All through this section, we'll give useful activities, models, and bits of knowledge to assist you with characterizing your own image and USP with clearness and conviction. Whether you're a carefully prepared business visionary or simply beginning on your part time job venture, the standards of individual marking will engage you to separate yourself, enhance your effect, and have an enduring impact on your crowd. In this way, as you leave on the most common way of characterizing your own image and extraordinary selling recommendation, recollect that credibility, consistency, and clearness are the foundations of compelling marking — directing you toward outcome in the packed commercial center of business.

Laying out an Internet based Presence Through Web-based Entertainment and Sites

In the present computerized age, laying out a vigorous web-based presence is fundamental for building major areas of strength for a powerful brand. In this section, we'll investigate the vital job that online entertainment and sites play in molding your image personality, associating with your interest group, and driving business development.

We'll start by looking at the meaning of online entertainment stages as amazing assets for brand building and local area commitment. From Facebook and Instagram to Twitter and LinkedIn, every stage offers remarkable open doors to exhibit your image character, share your story, and associate with possible clients. By choosing the stages that line up with your interest group and brand goals, you'll expand your compass and effect in the computerized scene.

Then, we'll dive into the method involved with making and advancing your web-based entertainment profiles to really mirror your image character. From making convincing bio depictions and profile pictures to organizing outwardly engaging substance and drawing in with your crowd, we'll give commonsense tips and systems to assist you with laying out major areas of strength for a reliable presence across the entirety of your web-based entertainment channels.

Yet, building a powerful internet based presence doesn't stop with web-based entertainment — it likewise reaches out to your site, which fills in as the computerized center point for your image. We'll investigate the fundamental parts of an expert and easy to understand site, including clear route, convincing visuals, and drawing in satisfied. By making a consistent and vivid internet based insight for your guests, you'll have an enduring impression and urge them to investigate further and draw in with your image.

All through this section, we'll stress the significance of consistency, legitimacy, and worth creation in building your web-based presence. By remaining consistent with your image character, conveying your extraordinary offer, and giving important substance and encounters to your crowd, you'll encourage trust, unwaveringness, and proclivity with your image.

Thus, as you leave on the excursion of laying out your internet based presence through web-based entertainment and sites, make sure to move toward each step with purposefulness, imagination, and a promise to greatness. By utilizing the force of computerized stages to intensify your image message and interface with your crowd, you'll establish major areas of strength for a point for progress and set up for long haul development and thriving.

Using Marking and Advertising Methods to Draw in Clients

In the clamoring commercial center of the present business world, viable marking and advertising methods are fundamental apparatuses for drawing in and holding clients. In this section, we'll investigate the workmanship and study of marking and promoting, furnishing you with the methodologies and experiences expected to hoist your image and charm your interest group.

We'll start by diving into the essentials of marking — characterizing your image personality, values, and character attributes that separate you from contenders. Through convincing narrating, visual components, and reliable informing, you'll figure out how to create a brand personality that reverberates with your crowd and encourages a profound association with your image.

Then, we'll investigate the job of advertising in enhancing your image message and arriving at your interest group actually. From conventional publicizing techniques to present day advanced showcasing procedures, we'll dig into the different methods and channels accessible for advancing your image and driving client commitment. Whether it's through web-based entertainment, email promoting, content promoting, or power-house organizations, you'll find an abundance of chances to interface with your crowd and exhibit the worth of your image.

In any case, powerful marking and showcasing go past arriving at your interest group — it's likewise about connecting with them on a more profound level and sustaining long haul connections. We'll investigate methods for building client dependability, requesting criticism, and encouraging a feeling of local area around your image. By focusing on consumer loyalty and conveying remarkable encounters at each touchpoint, you'll make brand advocates who are anxious to get the message out about your image and prescribe it to other people.

All through this part, we'll draw motivation from genuine models and contextual investigations of brands that have effectively utilized marking and advertising procedures to draw in and hold clients. By gaining from their triumphs and experiences, you'll acquire important insight and down to earth methodologies to apply to your own image building endeavors.

Thus, as you jump into the universe of marking and promoting, make sure to move toward every procedure with inventiveness, credibility, and a profound comprehension of your main interest group. By injecting your image with character, reason, and energy, you'll make an enduring impression and manufacture significant associations with your clients that reach out a long ways past exchanges.

Contextual analyses of Fruitful Side Tricksters Who Constructed Solid Brands

In the domain of business venture, there's a lot to gain from the encounters and triumphs of other people who have strolled the way before us. In this section, we'll dive into motivating contextual analyses of fruitful side tricksters who have incorporated flourishing brands as well as changed their interests into productive endeavors.

From the perspective of genuine models and accounts, we'll investigate the excursions of people who have explored the difficulties and wins of business with boldness, flexibility, and inventiveness. From solopreneurs and specialists to entrepreneurs and innovative experts, each contextual investigation offers exceptional bits of knowledge, examples, and motivation for hopeful side tricksters.

We'll analyze the procedures, strategies, and mentality moves that pushed these business visionaries to progress, from recognizing specialty potential open doors and utilizing their extraordinary assets to building connected with networks and encouraging brand reliability. By analyzing their marking and showcasing techniques, item contributions, and client commitment strategies, you'll acquire important insight and viable bits of knowledge to apply to your own innovative undertakings.

Yet, past the techniques and strategies, these contextual investigations offer something much more significant — the human stories behind the brands. You'll hear stories of energy, constancy, and reason — the main impetuses that pushed these business people to beat hindrances, challenge the chances, and transform their fantasies into the real world. Through their accounts, you'll track down motivation, inspiration, and consolation that achievement is conceivable, even despite misfortune.

As you submerge yourself for these situation studies, think about how their encounters reverberate with your own desires and difficulties. Consider the illustrations you can gather from their triumphs and disappointments, and how you can apply them to your own excursion of building areas of strength for an and flourishing second job.

In this way, as you venture through these rousing contextual investigations, recollect that achievement isn't an objective however an excursion

— a ceaseless course of getting the hang of, developing, and advancing as a business person. By drawing motivation from the individuals who have preceded you, you'll acquire the fortitude, intelligence, and assurance to graph your own way to progress and make a brand that leaves an enduring effect on the world.

5

Chapter 5: Managing Finances

Grasping Monetary Essentials and Planning

In the domain of business, monetary proficiency is the foundation of achievement. In this part, we'll set out on an excursion of understanding key monetary ideas and excelling at planning — a fundamental expertise for dealing with the funds of your side gig with certainty and clearness.

We'll begin by demystifying the essentials of money, from planning and income the executives to monetary preparation and objective setting. By acquiring a strong handle of these fundamental standards, you'll be better prepared to settle on informed conclusions about your business funds and explore the intricacies of business venture easily.

Then, we'll plunge into the universe of planning — an integral asset for following pay, costs, and reserve funds objectives. Whether you're dealing with a limited financial plan or making arrangements for development, making an individual and business financial plan gives a guide to monetary achievement, assisting you distribute assets really and focus on enjoying in arrangement with your objectives and needs.

As we investigate the complexities of planning, we'll examine techniques for overseeing income really — a basic part of monetary administration for side tricksters. By understanding the back and forth movement of pay and costs in your business, you'll be more ready to expect monetary difficulties, jump all over chances, and keep up with security and flexibility notwithstanding vulnerability.

In any case, past adjusting the books, viable monetary administration is likewise about anticipating what's to come. We'll dive into the significance of saving assets for both transient requirements and long haul objectives, like putting resources into business development, retirement investment funds, and crisis reserves. By embracing a proactive way to deal with monetary preparation, you'll establish the groundwork for monetary security and thriving both now and in the years to come.

All through this section, we'll give reasonable tips, devices, and strategies to assist you with becoming amazing at monetary administration and planning for your side gig. Whether you're simply beginning or hoping to take your business to a higher level, a strong comprehension of monetary essentials and planning is critical to accomplishing your pioneering yearnings and building a flourishing and maintainable business.

Setting Evaluating Systems and Overall revenues

Evaluating your items or administrations really is a urgent part of monetary administration for any side gig. In this section, we'll dive into the craftsmanship and study of setting evaluating methodologies and net revenues that guarantee productivity as well as mirror the worth you give to your clients.

We'll start by investigating the different elements that impact estimating choices, from creation expenses and contender evaluating to showcase interest and saw esteem. By understanding these elements and their interaction, you'll be better prepared to devise valuing methodologies that offset seriousness with productivity and reverberate with your ideal interest group.

Then, we'll examine strategies for computing overall revenues — a critical measurement for surveying the monetary soundness of your part time job. By understanding your expenses and income streams, you'll acquire experiences into your business' benefit and recognize amazing open doors for enhancing estimating and cost administration to expand benefits.

As we dig further into evaluating procedures, we'll investigate various methodologies, for example, cost-based estimating, esteem based valuing, and serious valuing. Every methodology offers one of a kind benefits and difficulties, and we'll give direction on choosing the most reasonable methodology in view of your plan of action, market elements, and client inclinations.

However, setting costs isn't just about amplifying benefits — it's likewise about conveying worth to your clients. We'll talk about techniques for conveying the incentive of your items or administrations successfully, guaranteeing that your evaluating mirrors the quality, uniqueness, and advantages you proposition to your clients.

All through this section, we'll give reasonable tips, models, and contextual analyses to assist you with exploring the intricacies of valuing your part time job really. Whether you're sending off another item, changing valuing for existing contributions, or investigating new business sectors, dominating evaluating procedures and net revenues is fundamental for making monetary progress and building a manageable business.

Overseeing Expenses and Lawful Contemplations

In the mind boggling scene of business, exploring charges and legitimate contemplations is a basic part of monetary administration for side hawkers. In this section, we'll set out on a complete investigation of the duty commitments, consistence necessities, and lawful contemplations that go with running a part time job.

We'll begin by acquainting you with the different duty commitments you might experience as a side trickster, from personal expenses and independent work charges to deals charges and permit to operate necessities. By understanding these commitments forthright, you'll be more ready to satisfy your duty obligations and keep away from likely punishments or liabilities.

Then, we'll dive into the different lawful designs accessible for side tricksters, like sole ownerships, associations, LLCs, and partnerships. Each construction offers special benefits and contemplations regarding obligation assurance, tax assessment, and authoritative prerequisites, and we'll give direction on choosing the most reasonable choice for your business needs and objectives.

As we investigate charge and legitimate contemplations, we'll examine systems for remaining coordinated with monetary records and documentation, guaranteeing consistence with charge regulations and guidelines, and planning for charge season actually. Whether you decide to deal with your duties autonomously or look for proficient help, remaining proactive and informed is vital to keeping away from normal traps and augmenting tax reductions.

Be that as it may, past consistence, overseeing charges and lawful contemplations is additionally about safeguarding your business and individual resources. We'll talk about methods for limiting dangers, for example, acquiring insurance inclusion, drafting policies and arrangements, and executing strategies and systems to protect against lawful debates and liabilities.

All through this section, we'll give viable tips, assets, and best practices to assist you with exploring the mind boggling scene of expenses and legitimate contemplations as a side trickster. Whether you're simply beginning or hoping to scale your business, remaining educated and proactive about charge and legitimate issues is fundamental for building a strong starting point for your enterprising undertakings.

Constructing and Keeping up with Monetary Strength

In the eccentric universe of business venture, building monetary strength is fundamental for enduring the unavoidable tempests and difficulties that might emerge along the way of running a part time job. In this part, we'll investigate procedures and strategies for bracing your monetary position, overseeing risk, and guaranteeing the drawn out manageability of your business tries.

We'll start by examining the significance of enhancing revenue sources — an essential rule of monetary versatility. By making various income streams inside your side gig, you'll spread risk and limit reliance on any single kind of revenue, expanding your soundness and versatility despite financial vacillations or market difficulties.

Then, we'll investigate the idea of making crisis reserves — a monetary wellbeing net that gives a support against unanticipated costs or slumps. Whether it's startling hospital expenses, hardware fixes, or a brief plunge in deals, having a monetary pad set up guarantees that you can explore through testing times without risking your business or individual budgets.

As we dig further into monetary versatility, we'll examine methods for safeguarding against chance and vulnerability, for example, getting protection inclusion, differentiating speculations, and carrying out risk the executives methodologies. By distinguishing possible dangers and creating emergency courses of action, you'll be more ready to moderate misfortunes and quickly return from difficulty with flexibility and certainty.

However, building monetary strength isn't just about getting ready for the most awful — it's additionally about anticipating what's to come. We'll investigate systems for laying out long haul monetary objectives, like retirement reserve funds, abundance aggregation, and heritage arranging. By embracing a proactive way to deal with monetary preparation, you'll make a guide for accomplishing your pioneering desires and getting your monetary future.

All through this section, we'll give pragmatic tips, assets, and contextual analyses to help you construct and keep up with monetary versatility in your side gig attempts. Whether you're simply beginning or hoping to develop your business, developing monetary versatility is fundamental for exploring the vulnerabilities of business venture and building a feasible and prosperous future for you as well as your business.

6

Chapter 6: Scaling Your Side Hustle

Evaluating Learning experiences and Development Techniques

Leaving on the excursion of scaling your side gig requires an essential way to deal with evaluate learning experiences and decide the most practical development techniques. In this section, we'll dig into the basic undertaking of assessing likely roads for development, understanding the advantages and difficulties related with each, and laying the basis for feasible extension.

We'll start by investigating the different learning experiences accessible to side tricksters, going from extending your item or administration contributions to entering new business sectors or broadening income streams. Every learning experience presents its own arrangement of benefits and contemplations, and we'll give bits of knowledge and guides to assist you with exploring the dynamic cycle actually.

As we dig further into learning experiences, we'll talk about the significance of directing statistical surveying and examination to evaluate request, contest, and market elements. By understanding the requirements and inclinations of your main interest group and distinguishing holes on the lookout, you'll be better prepared to gain by learning experiences and separate your second job from contenders.

Then, we'll investigate different development techniques, like natural development, vital associations, acquisitions, or diversifying. Every technique offers one of a kind benefits and difficulties, and we'll give direction on choosing the most reasonable methodology in light of your business objectives, assets, and hazard resistance.

In any case, surveying learning experiences isn't just about outer variables — it's additionally about assessing your inward abilities and preparation for extension. We'll talk about the significance of evaluating your group, framework, and functional cycles to guarantee they can uphold development really. By recognizing regions for development and tending to potential bottlenecks proactively, you'll establish a strong starting point for reasonable development and versatility.

All through this section, we'll give useful systems, instruments, and contextual investigations to assist you with surveying learning experiences and foster a masterful course of action for scaling your part time job. Whether you're hoping to develop your client base, venture into new business sectors, or send off new items or administrations, an exhaustive evaluation of learning experiences is fundamental for accomplishing your pioneering yearnings and building a flourishing and versatile business.

Utilizing Innovation and Computerization for Productivity and Adaptability

In the computerized age, innovation has turned into a crucial partner for side hawkers trying to scale their endeavors productively and reasonably. In this part, we'll investigate the extraordinary force of innovation and mechanization devices in smoothing out activities, further developing effectiveness, and empowering adaptability for your side gig.

We'll start by acquainting you with a heap of innovation arrangements that can reform your business tasks — from project the board programming and client relationship the executives (CRM) frameworks to online business stages and bookkeeping programming. These devices are intended to mechanize dull errands, smooth out work processes, and give important experiences that engage you to settle on information driven choices and upgrade your tasks for development.

Then, we'll dive into the key regions where innovation can greatestly affect your part time job's proficiency and versatility. Whether it's computerizing client interchanges, smoothing out request satisfaction processes, or dissecting promoting execution measurements, innovation offers vast opportunities for upgrading efficiency and lessening manual responsibilities.

Yet, embracing innovation arrangements isn't just about carrying out the most recent contraptions and programming — likewise about picking the right instruments line up with your business objectives and development plans. We'll talk about procedures for assessing innovation choices, choosing the most appropriate answers for your particular requirements, and incorporating them consistently into your current work processes.

As we investigate the advantages of innovation and computerization, we'll likewise address normal worries and difficulties, like expense contemplations, information security, and expectations to learn and adapt. By understanding these difficulties forthright and arranging as needs be, you'll be more ready to use innovation actually to drive proficiency, development, and development in your part time job.

All through this section, we'll give commonsense tips, assets, and contextual analyses to assist you with tackling the force of innovation and mechanization in scaling your second job. Whether you're a solopreneur or driving a group, embracing innovation is fundamental for remaining cutthroat, adjusting to change, and accomplishing your pioneering goals in the present speedy computerized scene.

Building a High-Performing Group and Designating Liabilities

As your part time job develops, so too does the requirement for a gifted and committed group to help its extension. In this section, we'll investigate the basic undertaking of building a high-performing group, selecting top ability, and designating liabilities successfully to engage your group and drive practical development.

We'll start by underscoring the significance of collecting a group that shares your vision, values, and energy for your second job. Whether you're recruiting consultants, project workers, or representatives, encircling yourself with roused and gifted people is fundamental for accomplishing your business objectives and keeping a positive organization culture.

Then, we'll examine methodologies for selecting and recruiting top ability, from making convincing sets of responsibilities to utilizing systems administration, references, and online stages to draw in qualified applicants. By taking on an essential way to deal with ability procurement, you'll build your possibilities tracking down an ideal choice for your group and expanding their commitments to your side gig's prosperity.

Be that as it may, building a high-performing group isn't just about enlistment — it's likewise about establishing a steady and cooperative workplace where colleagues feel esteemed, engaged, and inspired to succeed. We'll investigate methods for cultivating correspondence, trust, and fellowship among colleagues, as well as techniques for perceiving and remunerating their commitments.

As your group develops, successful designation of undertakings and obligations turns out to be progressively significant. We'll examine procedures for designating errands decisively, coordinating liabilities with colleagues' abilities and assets, and giving clear assumptions and input to guarantee responsibility and execution greatness.

All through this part, we'll give functional tips, devices, and contextual analyses to help you construct and deal with a high-performing group that drives economical development in your second job. Whether you're driving a little group or increasing your tasks, putting resources into your group's turn of events and strengthening is fundamental for accomplishing your pioneering desires and building a flourishing and tough business.

Creating Frameworks and Cycles for Supportable Development

As your second job extends and develops, laying out proficient frameworks and cycles becomes fundamental for overseeing intricacy, keeping up with consistency, and supporting development. In this part, we'll investigate the significance of creating vigorous frameworks and cycles and give direction on the best way to plan and carry out them actually.

We'll start by underlining the job of frameworks and cycles in working with reasonable development and versatility. By reporting work processes, normalizing techniques, and improving business tasks, you'll make a strong starting point for smoothing out errands, upgrading efficiency, and limiting blunders or shortcomings.

Then, we'll talk about functional methodologies for creating frameworks and cycles custom fitted to your part time job's interesting requirements and targets. Whether it's mechanizing dull errands, executing project the board apparatuses, or making normalized working strategies, we'll give experiences and guides to assist you with planning work processes that help your business objectives and drive productivity.

In any case, creating frameworks and cycles isn't just about making unbending designs — it's likewise about encouraging a culture of persistent improvement and transformation. We'll investigate procedures for requesting criticism from colleagues, observing execution measurements, and refining processes in view of experiences and learnings accumulated over the long run.

As your second job develops, it's fundamental to return to and refine your frameworks and cycles consistently to guarantee they stay successful and lined up with your advancing business needs. We'll talk about techniques for adaptability, for example, planning adaptable frameworks that can oblige development and extension without forfeiting proficiency or quality.

All through this section, we'll give functional structures, apparatuses, and contextual analyses to help you create and carry out frameworks and cycles that help manageable development in your part time job. Whether you're a solopreneur or driving a group, putting resources into the improvement of strong frameworks and cycles is fundamental for accomplishing your innovative yearnings and building a flourishing and versatile business.

7

Chapter 7: Transitioning to Your Main Hustle

Assessing Availability and Arranging the Progress

Setting out on the progress from a side gig to your principal hustle is a critical stage — one that requires cautious assessment of your preparation and fastidious wanting to guarantee a smooth and fruitful change. In this section, we'll direct you through the most common way of evaluating your status, both by and by and expertly, and creating a far reaching intend to explore this energizing yet testing venture.

We'll begin by leading an exhaustive assessment of your ongoing part time job's presentation and direction. This includes examining key measurements like income, client obtaining, and market interest to check the suitability and potential for development of your part time job. By understanding where your business stands today, you'll be better prepared to arrive at informed conclusions about progressing it into your primary hustle.

Then, we'll dive into the individual preparation factors that are fundamental for a fruitful change. This incorporates surveying your monetary readiness, risk resistance, and innovative outlook. We'll examine techniques for overseeing monetary dangers, fabricating a monetary wellbeing net, and developing the strength and assurance expected to explore the vulnerabilities of business.

With a reasonable comprehension of your status, we'll then direct you through the most common way of making a progress plan. This includes setting explicit achievements, courses of events, and key achievement markers to keep tabs on your development and guarantee you're on the correct way toward progressing to your principal hustle. Whether it's accomplishing sure income targets, getting financing, or creating fundamental functional cycles, a very much created progress plan fills in as your guide for progress.

All through this section, we'll give functional activities, instruments, and guides to assist you with evaluating your status and foster a progress plan that lines up with your objectives and yearnings. By adopting a key and proactive strategy to arranging the change to your fundamental hustle, you'll expand your odds of coming out on top and establish a strong starting point for building the matter of your fantasies.

Overseeing Dangers and Beating Difficulties

Changing from a second job to your fundamental hustle isn't without its dangers and difficulties. In this section, we'll investigate systems for distinguishing, moderating, and conquering the hindrances that might emerge en route, guaranteeing a smooth and fruitful progress to your new pursuit.

We'll start by distinguishing potential dangers related with the change cycle, from monetary vulnerabilities to functional difficulties and individual penances. By directing an extensive gamble evaluation, you'll acquire experiences into the possible entanglements and weaknesses that might influence your progress process.

Then, we'll talk about systems for dealing with these dangers actually. This incorporates creating emergency courses of action, getting reinforcement financing sources, and executing risk moderation methodologies to limit the effect of unexpected occasions or mishaps. We'll likewise investigate the significance of keeping a positive outlook and embracing vulnerability as a feature of the innovative excursion.

Be that as it may, overseeing gambles isn't just about getting ready for the most obviously awful — it's likewise about taking advantage of chances and transforming difficulties into benefits. We'll examine methods for remaining deft and versatile even with change, distinguishing open doors for development and development, and utilizing your assets to beat snags and arise more grounded on the opposite side.

All through this section, we'll give commonsense tips, contextual investigations, and genuine guides to delineate how business people have effectively overseen gambles and conquered moves during their change to their fundamental hustle. Whether it's exploring monetary requirements, defeating self-question, or tending to functional obstacles, flexibility and creativity are key ascribes that will assist you with beating difficulties and flourish in your new pursuit.

Building a Strong Starting point for Your Primary Hustle

As you change from a second job to your fundamental hustle, essential to lay out a strong groundwork will uphold the development and supportability of your new pursuit. In this section, we'll investigate the fundamental components that contain this establishment and give direction on the most proficient method to lay them actually.

We'll start by talking about the significance of laying out lawful and monetary designs for your primary hustle. This incorporates choosing the proper business element, like a sole ownership, association, LLC, or company, and enlisting your business with the important specialists. We'll likewise investigate methodologies for overseeing funds, getting subsidizing, and fostering a strong marketable strategy that frames your objectives, target market, serious scene, and development methodology.

Then, we'll dig into the marking and situating of your primary hustle. Building serious areas of strength for a personality and laying out an unmistakable offer are fundamental for drawing in clients, separating yourself from contenders, and building trust and validity in the commercial center. We'll examine procedures for characterizing your image's character, planning a convincing visual personality, and imparting your special offer really to your interest group.

Yet, building a strong groundwork goes past legitimate and marking contemplations — it likewise includes laying out functional cycles and frameworks that help your principal hustle's everyday exercises. We'll investigate techniques for setting up proficient work processes, advancing inventory network the board, and executing innovation arrangements that improve efficiency and adaptability.

All through this section, we'll give down to earth tips, assets, and contextual investigations to assist you with building a strong starting point for your principal hustle. Whether you're simply beginning or progressing a current second job into your full-time center, putting time and exertion into laying out areas of strength for a will deliver profits over the long haul, making way for supported achievement and development in your pioneering venture.

Taking the Jump: Executing Your Change Plan

After careful readiness and arranging, now is the right time to take the jump and execute your progress intend to transform your side gig into your fundamental hustle. In this part, we'll direct you through the functional parts of making this progress, from stopping your normal everyday employment to advising clients or clients and dealing with the close to home and mental parts of this critical life altering event.

We'll begin by talking about the execution of your progress plan, which might incorporate setting courses of events, achievements, and activity ventures for sending off your fundamental hustle. Whether it's getting funding, finishing item improvement, or formalizing associations, we'll give direction on executing each phase of your arrangement with accuracy and certainty.

Then, we'll investigate the calculated contemplations engaged with progressing from a part time job to your fundamental kind of revenue. This might incorporate leaving your normal everyday employment, advising clients or clients of your new concentration, and progressing liabilities or agreements easily to limit disturbance to your business activities.

In any case, past the useful angles, we'll likewise dive into the close to home and mental parts of taking the jump toward your fundamental hustle. This might include overseeing fears and questions, embracing vulnerability, and keeping fixed on your drawn out vision and objectives.

We'll examine methods for developing versatility, remaining inspired, and keeping a positive outlook during times of progress and change.

All through this part, we'll give experiences, stories, and genuine guides to outline how different business visionaries have effectively explored the progress from side gig to primary hustle. By drawing motivation from their encounters and applying the illustrations figured out how to your own excursion, you'll be more ready to take the jump with certainty and clearness, realizing that you have the right stuff, assets, and assurance to prevail in your new pursuit.

8

Chapter 8: Overcoming Challenges

Recognizing Normal Difficulties and Snags

In the turbulent excursion of business, difficulties and impediments are unavoidable associates. In this part, we set out on an excursion of investigation and contemplation, digging profound into the normal obstacles looked by business people on their journey for progress. By distinguishing and understanding these difficulties, we arm ourselves with the knowledge and versatility expected to explore the frequently slippery landscape of business possession.

We start by focusing on the most common difficulties experienced by business people, going from monetary imperatives and market immersion to savage contest and moving shopper inclinations. By perceiving the nature and greatness of these deterrents, we gain a more clear comprehension of the powers at play in the pioneering biological system and the potential road obstructions that might prevent our advancement.

Then, we dive into the underlying drivers and ramifications of these difficulties, analyzing their effect on business development, supportability, and individual prosperity. Whether it's wrestling with income issues, confronting dismissal from financial backers, or feeling overpowered by the requests of business venture, we investigate the mental, profound, and viable implications of these difficulties on our pioneering venture.

Be that as it may, in the midst of the affliction lies an open door. We uncover the bright sides concealed inside the billows of challenge, finding how deterrents can act as impetuses for development, advancement, and change. By reevaluating difficulties as any open doors for learning and variation, we engage ourselves to transcend misfortune and arise more grounded, savvier, and stronger than previously.

All through this section, we offer direction on creating strength and versatile methodologies to conquer deterrents and continue on even with misfortune. Drawing on bits of knowledge from brain science, business hypothesis, and genuine experience, we outfit ourselves with the devices and attitude expected to explore the unavoidable difficulties of business venture and arise triumphant on the opposite side.

Procedures for Versatility and Variation

In the powerful scene of business, flexibility and versatility are essential characteristics that can spell the distinction among progress and disappointment. In this part, we leave on an excursion of self-revelation and development, investigating the outlook moves and survival techniques that engage business visionaries to explore difficulties with beauty, certainty, and confidence.

We start by presenting the idea of strength — a characteristic that empowers people to return quickly from misfortunes, difficulty, and disappointment more grounded than previously. Through tales, research discoveries, and reasonable activities, we dig into the parts of strength, from mindfulness and profound guideline to good faith and steadiness. By developing these characteristics inside ourselves, we lay the preparation for enduring the hardships of business venture with versatility and beauty.

Then, we investigate the specialty of transformation — the capacity to turn, advance, and develop because of changing conditions and market elements. Drawing motivation from nature's versatile procedures, we reveal the standards of adaptability, readiness, and imagination that support effective variation in business. Whether it's embracing new advances, turning plans of action, or reconsidering item contributions, we find how versatility encourages development and impels us forward even with vulnerability.

Yet, strength and transformation don't happen in a vacuum — they require purposeful exertion and practice. We offer pragmatic methodologies for building versatility and encouraging flexibility in our regular routines, from care practices and stress the board strategies to looking for criticism, embracing disappointment, and developing a development mentality. By incorporating these systems into our enterprising excursion, we sustain ourselves against misfortune and position ourselves for long haul achievement and satisfaction.

All through this part, we share accounts of strength and variation from business people who have explored difficulties with mental fortitude, assurance, and imagination. Through their encounters, we gain experiences, motivation, and pragmatic insight to direct us on our own excursion of development and change. Outfitted with strength and versatility, we embrace the vulnerabilities of business venture with certainty and positive thinking, realizing that we have the ability to beat any deterrent that holds us up.

Looking for Help and Building an Encouraging group of people

In the frequently lone excursion of business venture, looking for help from others can be a signal of light in the haziness. In this part, we investigate the significant effect of building an encouraging group of people contained coaches, companions, and expert associations who can offer direction, support, and point of view during seasons of challenge and vulnerability.

We start by stressing the significance of looking for help from coaches — experienced people who can offer important bits of knowledge, astuteness, and guidance in light of their own pioneering venture. Whether through proper mentorship programs, organizing occasions, or special interactions, coaches act as believed guides who can assist us with exploring the intricacies of business venture and keep away from normal entanglements en route.

Then, we direct our concentration toward the force of friend support

— encircling ourselves with similar people who share our energy, aspiration, and vision for progress. Peer encouraging groups of people give a feeling of kinship, fortitude, and responsibility that can reinforce our flexibility and inspiration during testing times. By interfacing with individual business people, we get sufficiently close to an abundance of information, assets, and support that can assist us with defeating obstructions and accomplish our objectives.

Be that as it may, building an encouraging group of people isn't just about looking for counsel and direction — it's likewise about offering in return and adding to the progress of others. We investigate methodologies for sustaining corresponding connections inside our encouraging group of people, from offering mentorship and direction to sharing assets and open doors. By developing a feeling of liberality and cooperation, we encourage a local area of help that benefits all interested parties.

All through this section, we offer viable tips and procedures for building areas of strength for an organization that can support us through the ups and downs of business venture. Whether through proper mentorship programs, organizing occasions, or online networks, the help of others is a significant asset that can fuel our development, versatility, and progress in the pioneering venture.

Transforming Difficulties into Open doors for Development

In the midst of the hardships of business venture lies a strong truth: challenges can possibly be extraordinary impetuses for development and development. In this section, we set out on an excursion of reexamining misfortune as any open door, finding how mishaps and impediments can act as venturing stones to better progress and satisfaction.

We start by investigating the idea of disappointment not as a last objective, but rather as an important piece of the pioneering venture. By embracing disappointment as an instructor as opposed to an enemy, we open the way to important illustrations, experiences, and potential open doors for development. Through accounts of flexibility and steadiness, we witness how business visionaries have changed misfortunes into springboards for advancement and accomplishment.

Then, we dig into the craft of flexibility — the capacity to return from misfortune with reestablished strength, assurance, and innovativeness. Drawing motivation from brain research, neuroscience, and reasoning, we uncover the procedures and outlook moves that engage us to transcend difficulties and arise more grounded on the opposite side. By reexamining misfortunes as transitory mishaps as opposed to outlandish deterrents, we develop the flexibility expected to explore the ups and downs of business with effortlessness and strength.

Yet, strength alone isn't sufficient — we should likewise have the boldness to embrace change and take advantage of chances for development. We investigate the force of variation — the capacity to turn, advance, and develop because of changing conditions and market elements. By remaining light-footed, adaptable, and receptive, we change difficulties into open doors for development, imagination, and reevaluation.

All through this part, we offer useful procedures and activities for embracing disappointment, developing flexibility, and taking advantage of chances for development. Whether it's reevaluating misfortunes as growth opportunities, looking for criticism from coaches and companions, or investigating new roads for advancement, we find how difficulties can be changed into impetuses for individual and expert development. Equipped with versatility, mental fortitude, and a readiness to embrace transform, we rise out of misfortune more grounded, savvier, and more proficient than previously, prepared to vanquish the difficulties that lie ahead in the enterprising excursion.

9

∽

Chapter 9: Thriving as a Full-Time Entrepreneur

Embracing the Enterprising Outlook

Leaving on the excursion of full-time business requires something other than an act of pure trust — it requests a key change in mentality. In this section, we dive into the fundamental credits and outlook shifts important to flourish as a full-time business visionary, engaging you to embrace the difficulties and valuable open doors that lie ahead with certainty and strength.

We start by investigating the center qualities of fruitful business visionaries, from flexibility and versatility to innovativeness and diligence. By developing these traits inside yourself, you'll foster the flexibility expected to climate the unavoidable tempests of business venture and the versatility to turn and enhance in light of evolving conditions.

Then, we jump into the idea of a development mentality — the conviction that capacities and insight can be created through commitment and difficult work. By embracing a development mentality, you'll move toward difficulties as any open doors for learning and development, instead of unfavorable obstructions. We'll examine methods for reevaluating difficulties, embracing disappointment, and developing a feeling of interest and receptiveness to new encounters and valuable open doors.

However, outlook alone isn't sufficient — we should likewise develop the discipline and assurance expected to transform our enterprising vision into the real world. We investigate procedures for defining clear objectives, separating them into significant stages, and keeping on track and persuaded even with interruptions and mishaps. By adjusting our activities to our vision and values, we establish the groundwork for long haul achievement and satisfaction as full-time business people.

All through this part, we offer reasonable activities, bits of knowledge, and genuine guides to assist you with developing the pioneering mentality expected to flourish in the high speed and questionable universe of business. By embracing strength, flexibility, and a development outlook, you'll situate yourself for progress and satisfaction as you leave on the invigorating excursion of full-time business.

Using time productively and Efficiency Techniques

As a full-time business person, excelling at using time effectively and efficiency is fundamental for boosting your viability and accomplishing your objectives. In this part, we dig into the methodologies and strategies that will assist you with tackling your significant investment all the more effectively, permitting you to zero in on the main thing and push your business forward.

We start by investigating the significance of prioritization and objective setting in successful using time effectively. By recognizing your most significant errands and adjusting them to your drawn out targets, you can guarantee that you're effective financial planning your significant investment where it will have the best effect. We'll examine methods for laying out Brilliant objectives, stalling down into reasonable advances, and making a guide for progress.

Then, we investigate the force of schedules and organized plans in improving efficiency. Whether it's laying out a morning schedule to establish the vibe for the afternoon or carrying out time-impeding strategies to dispense committed time for centered work, schedules can give the construction and discipline expected to keep focused and gain significant headway toward your objectives.

However, overseeing time actually likewise requires a consciousness of normal efficiency traps, like dawdling, performing multiple tasks, and computerized interruptions. We'll talk about techniques for defeating these difficulties, from rehearsing care and limiting interruptions to carrying out innovation instruments and efficiency hacks that can assist you with keeping on track and useful over the course of the day.

At long last, we'll investigate the significance of keeping up with balance between serious and fun activities as a full-time business person. While commitment and difficult work are fundamental for progress, it's likewise vital to focus on taking care of oneself and personal time to forestall burnout and keep up with long haul prosperity. We'll talk about strategies for defining limits, overseeing pressure, and cutting out time for rest, unwinding, and significant associations beyond work.

All through this section, we'll give functional tips, instruments, and activities to assist you with dominating using time productively and efficiency as a full-time business visionary. By executing these procedures and strategies into your day to day everyday practice, you'll be better prepared to amplify your adequacy, accomplish your objectives, and track down satisfaction in the pioneering venture.

Exploring Vulnerability and Overseeing Pressure

In the turbulent universe of business venture, vulnerability and stress are dependable friends. In this part, we investigate systems for exploring the vulnerabilities and tensions of business while defending your psychological and close to home prosperity.

We start by recognizing the certainty of vulnerability in the enterprising excursion. Whether it's market changes, surprising difficulties, or the intrinsic dangers of beginning a business, vulnerability can bring out sensations of dread, uncertainty, and uneasiness. By embracing vulnerability as an intrinsic piece of the enterprising system, we can move our viewpoint and develop versatility despite affliction.

Then, we dig into pressure the executives strategies to assist you with adapting to the tensions of business. From care practices and profound breathing activities to customary activity and sufficient rest, we investigate procedures for overseeing pressure and advancing close to home prosperity. By focusing on taking care of oneself and integrating pressure decrease methods into your day to day everyday practice, you can moderate the adverse consequences of stress and keep up with balance in your life.

However, exploring vulnerability and overseeing pressure likewise requires a proactive way to deal with strength building. We examine procedures for building mental strength, for example, rethinking negative contemplations, looking for social help, and keeping a feeling of viewpoint in testing times. By developing flexibility, you can quickly return from mishaps more grounded than previously and face the hardships of business venture with effortlessness and certainty.

At long last, we investigate the significance of keeping a feeling of direction and importance in the enterprising excursion. By adjusting your activities to your qualities and vision, you can track down satisfaction and fulfillment in your work, even despite vulnerability and difficulty. We talk about procedures for remaining associated with your feeling of direction, whether it's through customary reflection, significant connections, or rewarding your local area.

All through this part, we give commonsense tips, activities, and genuine guides to assist you with exploring vulnerability and oversee pressure as a full-time business person. By embracing vulnerability, focusing on taking care of oneself, and remaining associated with your feeling of direction, you can flourish notwithstanding misfortune and track down satisfaction in the enterprising excursion.

Developing Long haul Achievement and Satisfaction

Past the everyday difficulties and prompt objectives of business lies the quest for long haul achievement and satisfaction. In this part, we investigate procedures for supporting achievement and tracking down satisfaction as a full-time business person throughout the span of your pioneering venture.

We start by looking at the significance of defining significant objectives that line up with your qualities, interests, and vision for what's to come.

By characterizing your meaning of progress and recognizing the main thing to you, you can make a guide for accomplishing your drawn out desires and tracking down satisfaction in your work.

Then, we dive into the idea of direction — the main thrust behind your pioneering tries. By developing a reasonable feeling of direction and adjusting your activities to your qualities and vision, you can implant importance and importance into your work, even notwithstanding difficulties and mishaps. We talk about methods for remaining associated with your feeling of direction, whether it's through normal reflection, significant connections, or rewarding your local area.

However, supporting achievement and satisfaction as a full-time business person likewise requires a sound outlook and point of view. We investigate methodologies for keeping an uplifting perspective, developing strength, and returning quickly from misfortunes more grounded than previously. By reexamining difficulties as any open doors for development and learning, you can explore the promising and less promising times of business venture with beauty and certainty.

At last, we examine the significance of balance between serious and fun activities in supporting long haul achievement and satisfaction. While commitment and difficult work are fundamental for accomplishing your objectives, it's additionally pivotal to focus on taking care of oneself and margin time to forestall burnout and keep up with prosperity. We offer functional tips and methodologies for defining limits, overseeing pressure, and cutting out time for rest, unwinding, and significant associations beyond work.

All through this section, we give bits of knowledge, activities, and genuine guides to assist you with developing long haul achievement and satisfaction as a full-time business person. By adjusting your activities to your qualities, remaining associated with your feeling of direction, and focusing on taking care of oneself, you can flourish in the enterprising excursion and track down satisfaction chasing after your fantasies.

10

～

Chapter 10: Conclusion

Considering Your Excursion

As we arrive at the finish of this extraordinary excursion, now is the ideal time to stop and consider the way we've voyaged — from the initiation of our side gig to the acknowledgment of our full-time enterprising undertaking. This section welcomes us to dive into thoughtfulness, praising our accomplishments, recognizing our difficulties, and evaluating the significant individual and expert development we've encountered en route.

We start by making space for appreciation and reflection, perceiving the achievements we've reached, the illustrations we've learned, and the versatility we've developed. Through journaling, self-reflection works out, and deliberate objective setting, we gain clearness and viewpoint on the exciting bends in the road of the enterprising excursion, appreciating the ups and gaining from the downs.

Considering our process permits us to praise our victories as well as to embrace our disappointments as significant learning open doors. Every misfortune, every obstruction, has been a venturing stone on our way to development and improvement. By recognizing and embracing these encounters, we extend how we might interpret ourselves and our enterprising excursion, arising more grounded and stronger than previously.

Yet, reflection isn't simply a review practice — it's likewise an impetus for future development and achievement. As we think back on our excursion, we reveal experiences and examples that illuminate our choices and techniques pushing ahead. We distil these critical important points into noteworthy experiences, laying the preparation for proceeded with development, advancement, and progress in our enterprising undertakings.

All through this part, we're welcome to take part in a course of profound reflection and appreciation, regarding the excursion we've voyaged and the examples we've learned. By embracing this snapshot of interruption and thoughtfulness, we set up for the following part of our innovative excursion, equipped with insight, flexibility, and a recharged feeling of direction and assurance.

Illustrations Learned and Key Focal points

As we close to the finish of our excursion, it's fundamental for stop and think about the priceless illustrations learned and bits of knowledge acquired en route. This part fills in as a storehouse for refining the embodiment of our enterprising experience, exemplifying the victories, challenges, and critical minutes that have molded our excursion from a second job to a full-time try.

We start by distinguishing and articulating the key illustrations advanced all through our pioneering venture. Whether it's finding the significance of flexibility despite misfortune, learning the specialty of compelling using time effectively, or leveling up our skill to adjust and improve in light of evolving conditions, every example fills in as a structure block in our development and improvement as business visionaries.

Then, we think about the triumphs and disappointments that have characterized our excursion, extricating experiences and intelligence from both. Triumphs certify our assets, approve our endeavors, and drive us forward with certainty and force. Disappointments, then again, offer important open doors for reflection, development, and course adjustment. By embracing the two victories and disappointments as vital pieces of the enterprising excursion, we develop a mentality of nonstop learning and improvement.

Yet, past individual examples and encounters, we additionally uncover all-encompassing topics and examples that have arisen all through our excursion. Whether it's the significance of versatility, the force of local area and encouraging groups of people, or the need of keeping a feeling of direction and vision, these subjects act as core values that illuminate our choices and activities as business people.

All through this part, we're welcome to take part in a course of profound reflection and contemplation, digging our encounters for bits of knowledge and shrewdness that will direct us on our future pioneering tries. By refining these examples learned and key action items, we arm ourselves with the information, flexibility, and assurance expected to explore the vulnerabilities and difficulties of business venture with beauty and certainty.

Laying out Future Objectives and Vision

As we stand at the edge of another part in our pioneering venture, now is the right time to graph a course for the future, defining aggressive objectives and making a convincing vision for progress and satisfaction. This part fills in as a guide for imagining the following period of our enterprising undertakings, adjusting our yearnings to our qualities, interests, and long haul targets.

We start by investigating the most common way of laying out future objectives — an essential move toward making an interpretation of our vision into noteworthy stages and achievements. By characterizing clear, explicit, and quantifiable objectives, we make a guide for progress that directs our activities and choices pushing ahead. We dig into procedures for laying out Shrewd objectives — objectives that are Explicit, Quantifiable, Feasible, Significant, and Time-bound — and investigate techniques for separating them into sensible advances.

Then, we direct our concentration toward creating a convincing vision for the future — a striking, motivating image of what achievement resembles for us as full-time business people. We investigate the significance of adjusting our own qualities, interests, and desires with our business objectives and goals, guaranteeing that our vision mirrors our credible selves and resounds profoundly with our feeling of direction.

In any case, laying out future objectives and vision isn't just about thinking beyond practical boundaries — it's likewise about making a down to earth plan for accomplishing those fantasies. We examine methods for making a dream load up, envisioning our objectives, and fostering a guide for progress that frames the activities, assets, and courses of events expected to transform our vision into the real world.

All through this section, we're welcome to dream strongly and imagine the future we longing for us as well as our organizations. By defining clear objectives, making a convincing vision, and making a guide for progress, we establish the groundwork for proceeded with development, development, and satisfaction in our enterprising excursion. Outfitted with clearness, reason, and assurance, we leave on the following period of our pioneering attempts with idealism and certainty.

Embracing the Following Part

As we finish up this extraordinary excursion, we stand near the precarious edge of another section loaded up with boundless conceivable outcomes and open doors. This last section fills in as a source of inspiration — a suggestion to embrace the following period of our enterprising excursion with good faith, versatility, and assurance.

We start by recognizing the continuous idea of business venture — the steadily advancing scene, the consistent difficulties, and the unlimited potential for development and advancement. While this excursion might have arrived at its decision, the innovative soul inside us stays alive and energetic, driving us forward with energy and reason.

Then, we ponder the examples took in, the bits of knowledge acquired, and the individual and expert development experienced all through this excursion. Each victory, every mishap, has been a venturing stone on our way to turning into the business people we were intended to be. By embracing the examples of the past, we position ourselves for outcome later on, equipped with insight, strength, and a restored feeling of direction.

Yet, past reflection lies activity. We're urged to move forward, seeking after our objectives and dreams with boldness and assurance. Whether it's starting another endeavor, extending a current business, or chasing after new open doors for development and development, we approach the future with a feeling of energy and plausibility.

At last, we're helped to remember the significance of remaining associated with our feeling of direction, keeping up with balance between fun and serious activities, and tracking down bliss and satisfaction chasing after our fantasies. As we leave on this new section, we focus on supporting our prosperity, cultivating significant connections, and remaining consistent with ourselves and our qualities.

All through this part, we're welcome to embrace the following section of our innovative excursion with open hearts and receptive outlooks. By embracing change, remaining strong, and remaining consistent with our vision, we position ourselves for proceeded with development, achievement, and satisfaction in the astonishing excursion ahead.